Vivian Nikanov

COOL COS

COOL COS

THE STORY OF
BILL COSBY

JOEL H. COHEN

SCHOLASTIC BOOK SERVICES
NEW YORK • TORONTO • LONDON • AUCKLAND • SYDNEY • TOKYO

Cover photos courtesy of National Broadcasting Company

Other photos courtesy of National Broadcasting Company, Temple University, the Sutton Public Relations Company, and Warner Brothers-Seven Arts.

6th printing February 1972   Printed in the U.S.A.

CONTENTS

On acting: "You've got to steer, keep the car straight, hit the brake right. First time you hit the brake, you know how the car stopped and almost flipped over? That's acting. Well, the more you drive, if you're a sensible person, the better you are. . . ."

About slapstick comedy: "I love Buster Keaton. I met Buster before he died. And I suppose it was one of the great moments as far as people taking advantage of being a celebrity."

INTRODUCTION

This book is about . . .

. . . a once poor ghetto youngster who now earns more money in a single week — sometimes in one night — than most people do in a year.

. . . a former shoeshine boy whose entertainment talents bring him earnings in the millions, but who speaks of giving it up in the next few years.

. . . a two-time school dropout who wants to be a teacher.

. . . a one-time bartender who doesn't drink.

. . . a funnyman who became a prize-winning actor.

. . . a Negro comedian who doesn't use racial material but who became a pioneering "Jackie Robinson of TV."

This book is about Bill Cosby, who is all these things, and more — a man of exceptional talent, enormous popularity, wide interests, and as many contrasts as writers of travel articles like to ascribe to distant lands.

It isn't the whole story. Cosby, a performer with a public of millions, is essentially a private person. And he has built a comedy career out of the blocks of his childhood, so that it's not always possible to distinguish what actually happened in his life from what his fertile imagination escalated into laugh-getting routines.

Still, it all belongs, and even the make-believe helps shed light on the real Bill Cosby — and what makes him tick, what turns him on, what bugs him, and who and what shaped him as an entertainer and human being.

This, then, is Cool Cos. . . .

Joel H. Cohen

How did his third mustache go over with the ladies? "I don't care about the ladies," he insisted, "I bucked my wife, man. I did. I fell in love with it. Looked like an old walrus, an old gunfighter . . . like Groucho Marx."

1

BILL AND EMMY

SHARING THE SPOTLIGHT

It's the evening of May 22, 1966. In glittering halls in Hollywood and New York City, some of the most famous names in show business have gathered to help the television industry honor its own.

It's the night of the Emmys, and a coast-to-coast TV audience shares the glamour and the excitement of guessing who will win the sometimes controversial awards that TV people crave the way movie stars do Oscars or home run sluggers the Most Valuable Player awards.

Now they've reached the category of "outstanding continued performance by an actor in a leading role in a dramatic series."

"The winner is . . ."

". . . Bill Cosby!"

As the audience applauds enthusiastically, Cosby, in New York, moves to accept his trophy. A tall, ruggedly good looking Philadelphian, the young comedian has been a cheerful, light-hearted cohost of the Emmy ceremonies. Now he turns serious. Well aware of the factors behind his triumph, Cosby pays tribute to NBC for "having the guts" to have signed him to costar in a regular nationally televised series, the first Negro ever given that opportunity.

Then, with deep emotion, he declares:

"I extend my hand to a man by the name of Robert Culp. He lost this because he helped me," Cosby says in a husky voice.

Those present understood. For Cosby had never acted professionally before *I Spy*, and, in an industry not especially celebrated for unselfishness, Culp, his costar, had patiently worked with Cosby to help him develop from a poor actor into a better-than-average dramatic performer, good enough (at least as a sentimental favorite) to win the award for which Culp himself was a contender.

People who knew Cosby were not surprised. It figured that Cosby the comic would win his gamble with serious acting. And it figured that he would share his moment in the spotlight — give appropriate credit and "tell it like it is" about how he got there.

For though Cosby liked to speak of himself as a "conman," he has earned a reputation as honest and sensitive, sincere and outspoken, fairly complex as well as funny, with a lot more going for him than his comic sensibilities. The soft-spoken, cool cat has deep emotional tides coursing beneath his casual surface.

Where did it begin? As he says in one of his record album titles, *I Started Out as a Child*.

2

FAT, WEIRD, BOWLEGS, AND JUNEBUG

THE GANG

Almost from the moment William Henry Cosby, Jr., made his world debut at about 3 a.m., July 12, 1937, in Germantown Hospital, North Philadelphia, Pennsylvania, he showed signs of "wonderfulness."

The oldest of four sons born to Anna and William Henry Cosby, Sr., Bill "matured" early — walking, talking, and teething well before others of the same age. By the time he was eight and one-half months old — when most children just crawl or toddle — the future track star was already running.

And without realizing it, he was off and running on his career — living the childhood that would be the raw material for his polished comic routines . . . playing the games, battling the fears, doing the mischief that he would later jokingly exaggerate into a multi-million dollar success.

Bill once said his career as a comedian really started

"The most important thing is how well you throw a forward pass."

at age three or four when he would "con" his mother out of a cookie. ("You know she'll say 'no' the first time you ask, but you know that if you can get her to laughing you can get around her.")

Bill Cosby grew up in a black ghetto in North Philadelphia, but his heart lived in the worlds of sports and entertainment.

Joe Louis and Ray Robinson, Jackie Robinson, Buddy Young, and the whole Harlem Globetrotter basketball team were among his heroes, and he was a dedicated radio fan of the Green Hornet, Lone Ranger, Jack Armstrong, Tom Mix, and all of the comedy shows.

Not surprisingly, early in his life Bill wished he could become an athlete and a comedian.

He wanted to do funny things partly because he felt that when people laughed at him, "that meant they liked me, they accepted me." (Later he'd add: "It was even better when they started throwing money.")

Bill was "always throwing lines," his brother Bob said, "even when we were kids playing touch football in the street."

He put some of his good lines into writing, as when, pretending to be his mother, "Shorty" (now an imposing six-footer) wrote a letter to a muscle-building company that had been demanding payment for equipment he ordered. Bill wrote: "William is only eight years old and he's crazy, so don't send any more stuff to him."

Money was always in short supply in the Cosby household, but Bill and his brothers had the necessities. They ate regularly, and while their clothing wasn't expensive, their mother saw to it that it was clean.

In Mrs. Cosby's opinion, Bill was always "a good boy, a lovely, warm, tender-hearted person." He comments: "All in all, I never really stepped too far out of line, because I was always afraid of my mother crying, embarrassing her or something like that."

About his childhood, Bill said, "Some of it was happy, some of it was pretty sad. The sad things I don't like to talk about at all. But I like to think about the groovy things we did."

One of the groovy things was trying to outwit the lifeguard at the public swimming pool, which had "rounds" — limited periods of time, usually an hour, that one group of youngsters could use the pool before having to make room for another. "The big thing to do," Bill recalled, "was to try to make all the rounds. But the lifeguard was pretty slick. He'd feel your trunks and if your trunks were wet, he wouldn't let you in."

According to Bill's mother, if Bill couldn't be the center of attraction he was unhappy. "The more people gathered around him, the better." Several of those who did gather around him were the boys he's immortalized in his routines:

— Fat Albert ("he used to be the fattest guy in our neighborhood; we just called him Fat Albert").

— Weird Harold ("You never even bothered with guys' names. Like we had a guy named Bowlegs and it was a long, long time before anybody found out his real name was Rufus Smith. And he was actually pigeontoed.")

— Junebug ("I knew his real name because he was in my class.")

The boys had their occasional fights, but as Bill remembers them, "they weren't spectacular things. You hit a guy and if he cried, that was it."

Bill and his cronies played the usual games — baseball, softball, basketball, football — but they had some favorite pastimes of their own, such as going to the city dump to hunt for rats.

They adapted most of their games to their concrete environment on the stoop, they played step baseball, a game in which the "hitter" bounces the ball off the front steps for singles or doubles, etc., depending on where it hits. In the schoolyard, Bill and his buddies played half-ball, a game whose object is to hit half a rubber ball with a broomstick. And they played buck-buck (in some cities, Johnny on a Pony), which he describes as a "game you play with your body. Guys line up and you pile a certain number of guys on until they collapse."

Often the boys' ballfield was the street, with football the most popular game. A quarterback's instructions from one of Cosby's routines — "Arnie, go down 10 steps and cut left to the black Chevy; Cosby, you go down to Third Street, catch the J bus, have him open the doors at 19th Street and I'll fake her to ya" — is only a slight exaggeration of the huddle strategy they employed to take advantage of existing "field" conditions.

In his neighborhood, Bill said, "the most important thing was how well you threw a forward pass."

"I was a carefree kid who was more or less unaware of the responsibilities of getting an education. . . . And if your mother is hip, you don't have to scrub any floors or make up your bed or anything like that, so that leaves all the time in the world for you to chase the ball."

3

PURPLE PANCAKES

THE MAN OF THE HOUSE

But life certainly wasn't all fun and games for Bill.

When he was 8, he suffered the immense shock of losing his oldest brother, James, 6, to rheumatic fever. "I was kind of prepared for it, though," Bill said. "I really didn't get to see him that much, he was always in the hospital."

Then one day, when Bill was 9, his father, who had held a variety of jobs as a laborer ("he was cool; he'd come back when the bills were paid") announced to the family that he had decided to make the Navy a career. As a ship's steward, he would be away from home most of the time.

"This," he told Bill, "means you're the man of the house."

His father was hardly gone when Bill turned to his brothers, Russell, then about three and one-half, and Bob, an infant and obviously too young to understand, and declared in a young but no-nonsense tone:

19

"I'm the man of the house now, you have to obey me."

And, according to their mother, as the years went by, they did.

With his father away and Mrs. Cosby at work, Bill sometimes had to be not only the man of the house, but the part-time mother, and he washed and ironed clothes and even cooked to help out. Bill liked to make popcorn, spaghetti and meatballs, and waffles. Tired of looking at the same old waffles, he put food coloring in the batter. "I dug them. I liked purple waffles, green, orange, red waffles. I loved them and I couldn't understand why my mother never dug them."

Often he had to baby-sit for his brothers and, like any typical youngster, tried not to let his duties interfere with his playing.

"I used to try to put them to sleep — give them a lot of cough medicine," he joked. He'd give his baby brother a bottle and burp him, then build up boxes and chairs around the bed to keep the infant from falling out. Once his charges were asleep, he'd go out and play ball, and when it wasn't his turn at bat, he'd run by to peek in at the boys through the window of their first floor apartment.

One day he thought his brothers were sleeping, but came back to find "they had a nice little fire going in the kitchen and were sitting around burning paper." Another time young Russell tried to make some biscuits with flour and water and burned the pan. When Mrs. Cosby came home, the boys feigned ignorance, but the smell in the house was too much and finally she asked what happened. In wide-eyed innocence, Bill said, "A man came in here and was trying to cook."

Imaginary men would show up again.

One of Cosby's most recent albums is titled, *To Russell, My Brother, Whom I Slept With,* and the fact is that he did indeed sleep with Russell and sometimes with Bob, too.

In one story he tells, the boys jump on the bed until it collapses. And when their father angrily bursts into the room demanding an explanation, Bill, looking as if butter wouldn't melt in his mouth, says "a man came through the window and started jumpin' on the bed till it broke."

When his father declares, "There's no window in this room," Bill shoots back, "He brought it with him."

Again, his mouth open, eyes gazing heavenward, Bill swears he's innocent of tormenting his younger brother, whom he has convinced they are surrounded by turtle heads. Their father says, in exasperation, "When I'm late for work in the morning, they'll understand I was killin' turtle heads."

Dad never could understand him, Bill tells an audience, but "Mom was groovy — she'd cry over anything. Find a piece of wood. 'That's beautiful,' she'd cry."

Speaking seriously, Bill told one interviewer, "If your old man was home a lot, that meant he wasn't working and things were tough. If your old man had something steady, like my Dad, it usually meant he had to be away from home so you didn't see him much. Either way, it was a hard thing for boys growing up."

It was especially hard for younger brothers — at least in the Bill Cosby stories of how he used to provoke his brother to tears. After repeated warnings such as "This is my side of the bed and I don't want your body touching it," he'd add the clincher: "You're not really my brother anyway. You were brought here by the police. They found you in a sewer hole, and they said Mom and Dad could keep you until you start lying." Their father comes in to console, "You'll always be my son and you can live here as long as you have a job."

"There was a little rivalry because of the age difference, I guess," Bill recalled about his relationship with his brothers, five and a half and nine years younger. "We had our little fights and our differences about things like who had the bigger piece of pie, who ate two pieces of cake and, later on, about property (guys borrow your clothes, stay on the phone, stuff like that)."

But there was also a tremendous mutual affection that has carried through the years.

Hearing stories about the Cosby boys and their excursions into accidental arson and wild story-telling, you might get the impression that Mrs. Cosby always had the strap out, but Bill said "Very seldom did our mother ever hit us."

Chewing out, yes. And "Oh, she'd cry, man . . . . "Whenever we goofed she cried. No spankings. No beatings. Her tears alone would shake us up. She'd start crying and you'd start crying. . . ."

Sometimes he cried on his own. One Christmas was a particularly teary occasion for Bill. A year or two before, the Cosbys had had no tree, "a fantastic kind of blow" to Bill. A year or two later, there *was* a tree, but no toys, no roller skates, no games. His mother handed him a five-dollar bill, which was a lot of money in their family, but to him this meant nothing. "Where's my present?" he wanted to know. Crying, he told his mother he would have been satisfied with anything, even an old candy bar, just so long as it was "something wrapped up, a gift, not just an old bill."

One gift Mrs. Cosby apparently did pass on to her oldest boy was an interest in stories.

A woman with a great concern about education, Mrs. Cosby would regularly read to her sons, usually at bedtime. "She'd read and we'd drop off," Bill remembers. She'd read from the Bible (maybe Bill's comic account of the dialogue between God and Noah began to form then); stories of Mark Twain — "she scared us half to death with those kids going down into that cave."

Drowsy or not, Bill couldn't help but be influenced. "For some reason, I was a pretty good reader."

His favorite reading matter as a child, though, was comic books. "I love them." He still has a grudge against a Philadelphian named Seymour who committed a pretty horrible crime. It wasn't so much the crime that offended Bill but the fact that "they went up to Seymour's house and found all those comic books and they said 'no more books like Seymour's been reading.' I got mad at Seymour because he took away all the groovy comic books."

More than one comic book hero has inspired Cosby comedy. Bill does a bit about mild mannered Clark Kent stepping into a phone booth to strip down to his Superman costume. A policeman who sees him demands, "Hey, fella, what are you doin' in there?"

"I'm changing clothes."

"You can't change in a phone booth. Who do you think you are?"

"I'm Superman."

"Sure, bring the wagon, Charley."

"If parents are bigoted, the children shouldn't listen to them.
It's the only time I would really say it.... We have extremists
in both cases, and I must excuse the black extremists because
they're only doing what they learned from the white extremists
and showing that they don't trust any more."

4

ORANGE CRATES AND
DREAM CASTLES

ODD JOBS

Like many a ghetto youngster, Bill had his share of odd jobs. Many of the boys, Bill included, would make empty orange crates into shoeshine boxes and go downtown where there were people who could afford shines. Bill always stopped when he had made two dollars. He'd take the money home to his mother, keep a quarter for himself, or let her decide how much spending money to give him.

One time, when he was giving his mother money, the shoeshine boy/man of the house made an eager promise:

"All the places Daddy didn't take you, when l grow up, I'm gonna take you. And all the things he couldn't, I'm gonna give you all that."

Bill worked in a grocery store, carrying sweet potatoes and collard greens out, setting up the vegetable stand, dusting off the cans. But he never got to cut the meat or count the money. "I worked from six in the morning till six at night, and six in the morning till eight at night Fridays and Saturdays, and got eight dollars a week" for the seven-day-a-week job.

Bill also had a job at a drugstore soda fountain, but "When it was time to dust off the pharmaceutical bottles, I moved them around and the guy didn't know where his bottles were, so he let me go."

When he wasn't working or going to school, he'd usually be playing ball. "If you found him home on a Sunday night," said brother Bob, "it would be because of a favorite comedian on TV. He'd wait to see him."

Sunday mornings were something else again: church.

Although his mother regularly took Bill to Sunday School at Hosley Temple, CME Church in Nicetown, Philadelphia, his church-going days are essentially memories and material for his comic view of life.

"I was a very wicked child," he'll say. "I had a praying mantis that I converted to an agnostic."

When Bill was born the family lived on Beechwood St. In a few years, they moved to Steward Street, also in the Germantown section of North Philadelphia, and then, not long after, to the first floor apartment in the Richard Allen Homes public housing project, where the Cosbys remained about 12 or 13 years. The move to the present family home was made about 1954.

There, at last, Bill had a room to himself, and he decorated it with pictures of movie stars and banners, trophies he'd won for excellence in athletics, and signs that bore such funny sayings as "Do unto others before they do unto you" and "Last week I couldn't even spell salesman; today I are one."

5

A LEFT-BACK HALFBACK

KING KOKO FROM KOO-KOO ISLAND

"You should either be an actor or a lawyer — you lie so good."

This was the evaluation of Bill Cosby's talents he remembers being given by Mrs. Paul A. Nagle (then Miss Mary B. Forchic), his sixth-grade teacher, who probably said it with better grammar.

For she, perhaps more than any other of his teachers, was "on" to the bright youngster who, by his own admission, never really studied. ("I did just enough so that I could give a little *conmanship* as to what I had done in homework.")

"She had the whole personality, she was beautiful," he said.

"I chased the ball, I guess, for 20 years, without worrying about the books and, as a result, wound up almost uneducated, except for a couple of teachers who embarrassed me in one way or another so that I did my homework."

"Some part of me will always want to go back to school and teach—not because I was once a dropout and have a lesson to teach, but because the one kid who could have gone the other way but who changed his mind is worth everything."

One of the teachers was Mrs. Nagle, now of Washington, D.C. ("She was quite militant," he joked about her use of a ruler.) Another was Miss McKinney. "She tried," he said. "She took me to the ballgame a couple of times, bought me some hot dogs and talked to me about studying, but she didn't do it either — make that impression — nor did Mrs. Nagle.

"I knew through pain and I felt embarrassed about what I was doing, but I still couldn't see it. Life was still a whole lot of play."

Bill's checkered school career began with kindergarten at Reynolds Elementary School. The only good thing about kindergarten, he says in one of his routines, "is that it teaches you how to say good-bye to your parents without crying." On opening day, the kindergartners are bawling with fear, "Oh, we're gonna die." But the next day, little boy Bill is the height of cool. In a very man-of-the-world voice, he says: "Good-bye, mother. Take care of yourself, won't you dear. I should be home, oh, 12:30, quarter to 1, maybe later. I might have a little milk with the boys."

Bill made it through kindergarten unscarred (he got an A in trips to the bathroom). Then he went to Mary Channing Wister School, where he sat in front of crying Charley.

There, as Mrs. Nagle remembers it, Bill came into her two-year class of "unreachable and unteachable" fifth and sixth graders with a reputation as a clown, high native intelligence, and a record of flunking just about all his courses. When he left after sixth grade, he was rated "outstanding" (the highest possible rating) in almost every subject, and Mrs. Nagle told Bill he had the ability to be just about anything he wanted.

Mrs. Nagle wrote on a paper or an early report card of Bill's, "In this classroom, there is one comedian and it is I. If you want to be one, grow up, get your own stage, and get paid for it." Another time she commented: "William would rather be a clown than a student and feels it is his mission to amuse his classmates in and out of school."

A strict disciplinarian, she nevertheless let the children tell jokes and this may be where Bill had his first opportunity to amuse a seated audience.

Mrs. Nagle gave Bill the lead role in such class operettas as *King Koko from Koo-Koo Island*, *Back to the Simple Life*, and *Tom Tit Tot*.

"I don't know how to act," he told her when she first picked him to star.

"You've been acting since you got here," she replied.

Bill still protested. "I don't think I can memorize the lines."

"Don't think about it. Memorize."

And so Bill not only memorized hundreds of lines, but sang (according to his teacher, "His voice wasn't great, but he could belt out a song") and danced among sticks that were clicked together by supporting players.

"If somebody would pick me for the play I would go ahead and do it, but if they said, 'We want volunteers for it,' I never volunteered," he recalled.

But if he was reluctant about volunteering for musical productions, he now remembers them with pleasure. "That was where I would really shine, man. You just put me on a stage, and after I got to feel my way around, you couldn't stop me. I was a ham — a ham and a half."

Bill shone in other ways, too. He became captain of

the track and baseball teams and was elected president of his class.

"He had a facility for getting to know people," Mrs. Nagle remembered, and although he was "a rough and tumble boy . . . he never hurt anybody, physically or verbally." Bubbling with humor, he was never rude.

He had an excellent attendance record and was good in all his subjects. In Mrs. Nagle's opinion he was now "marvelous in reading . . . did great work in math . . . was fascinated by social studies and world conditions." By the end of sixth grade, she was convinced he was college material and could certainly win a scholarship.

But life, he recalled, "was still a whole lot of play and I refused to accept the responsibility. I don't know what I even had in mind; it wasn't that I was going to be a professional football player or professional baseball player, or an artist or a drummer — it's just that I wanted to play; I wanted to have quote unquote fun.

"The one thing she said to me when I graduated sixth grade (because I had scored the highest in my room on the IQ test — it could have been 32, I don't know) was 'you're a very intelligent young man, but you should be working at it.' "

Still, sports occupied most of Bill's interest. At Fitz-Simons Junior High, which Bill attended after Wister, he was made captain of the tumbling team. His main qualification? "I had a funny run that made people laugh."

In junior high, there was one girl he had a crush on, and she supposedly liked him, "but we never got together because she was always going with somebody else."

Actually, girls weren't much on his mind until high school, and he didn't start "going out" with girls until "I had some money. We never really took girls out. I never had the money or the clothes to do it," Bill said. Instead, they went to parties. "You could dress up any old way to go to a party 'cause they turn the lights out and they can't see your pants don't match."

Outside of school he was playing on basketball and baseball teams. For the Philadelphia Bombers (formerly the Brown Bombers) he pitched a couple of games and then moved to second base. In his early teens, he hurled for a Police Athletic League club.

After Fitz-Simons, Bill won his way into Central High School, an all-boys school for gifted applicants with an IQ of at least 120. In later years Bill would reminisce about how bad he was in shop, how everything he made turned out looking like an ash tray. Was he really that bad? "Oh, yeah," he replied. "Mechanical drawing and shop — forget it."

There were aspects of his education at Central High he probably would like to forget. He broke his arm in the first football game he played for the school. And he was left back in the 10th grade there for two years.

Bill wasn't above sparing his mother the trouble of having to sign his report card. "He had us believing he was getting a good report," she said with a smile, "but he was flunking all his subjects."

"I think the only things I passed at Central were art and gym class," he said.

Finally, he got a transfer — to Germantown High. Invited back nine years later to receive a plaque, he explained to the Germantown High assembly why he had wanted to leave Central.

"I wasn't having any fun and I wasn't passing," he said. "I put in for a transfer to Germantown, where they had some girls at least."

His main pursuits at Germantown, he told the assembly, were coasting along and "being the class nut." He said, "I used to give the teachers fits, asking questions like 'What is air?' and forging passes."

At Germantown he played football and was the Bears' leading ground-gainer, ran track, starring in the high jump, and captained both teams. But then at 19, too old for high school track competition, he decided to quit school "because it was embarrassing. I was getting old, man. The kids looked like little kids and I was an old guy. I said 'let me out of here.'"

And, in 1956, out he got.

6

"DOC"

THE GRADUATE

Like many a high school dropout, Bill went into military service. After playing ball and working in a shoe repair shop and a car muffler manufacturing plant, he enlisted in the Navy and spent four years seeing not so much the world but himself. By the time his hitch was up, he had a better idea of the life he wanted and what he'd have to do to achieve it.

Bill's assignment as physical therapist took him to Bainbridge, Maryland; Quantico, Virginia; Bethesda, Maryland; Argentina; Newfoundland; and the Philadelphia Naval Hospital. He made it to Guantanamo Naval Base in Cuba on, "believe it or not, an LSD," said the comedian, who has never had to rely on drugs to "turn on." (LSD then stood for Landing Ship Dock.)

Meanwhile, he had learned the joy of healing, developed as a track athlete, and faced up to the hard realities of what the outside world would be for a young Negro without a high school diploma.

"I've never taken pills or smoked pot, no LSD or anything.
So I'm in pretty good shape.

The service took Bill away from his family physically, but in spirit he was as close to his mother and brothers as ever. Bill sent money and letters, and he'd come back home on leave to North 21st Street with watches or other gifts for Russell and Bob, extra spending money for his mother — and once a thick mustache for himself.

Bill's decision to enlist in the Navy naturally was upsetting to his mother, but his letters, especially the exaggerated accounts of boot camp, were amusing and reassuring. His mother found them "touching and warm."

One letter-writing quirk of his during his service days was to send his brother Bob's letters back to him graded, with spelling and grammar mistakes marked the way a teacher would ("sp" for spelling, etc.). "This was a pretty good letter, you get 83" might be the comment on one of them.

Did he do it as a gag? "No," said Bill. "I used to send them back with his mistakes because Bob's a good athlete and I knew he'd want to go to college, and the only way to do it is kind of to stay on him. Maybe I was a little too hard on him. . . ." (Bob, who starred in football at Germantown High, now attends Delaware State University.)

Bob and Russell agree that perhaps Bill sometimes took his responsibilities as the man of the house too seriously to suit them. Yet, Bob added, "he didn't leave home to go into service until we had shaped up. He kept us in line, kept after us on our studies, got angry if our grades weren't good or if we did anything to disturb our mother."

Bill explained, "I have a great sense of humor as far

as other people are concerned outside, but with people I love, if they don't do what I think is right, then I become very sarcastic. And that's hard to take. Most of the folks in my family, I think, have this biting sense of humor. If you're out of line, man, they can just drop it right on you. And it's just as dry as sawdust but it just goes so deep into the wound."

Actual physical wounds were to become a deep concern of Bill's as a Navy corpsman and physical therapist.

He'll make jokes about the GI medic who refuses to leave his foxhole to aid a wounded buddy because "I don't make house calls." But he was serious about the work he did in the Navy.

"It's a great, great field," he said of physical therapy. "A guy could come to you as your patient and be flat on his back, and a year or months later, perhaps walk out with braces. It's a great moment."

Bill used to look at the paraplegics and "wonder what I'd be like if I didn't have my arms or legs. I always tried to make them laugh. Lord knows, the way the world is today, we could all use a few laughs."

His recollections of his days as a therapist are varied:

— Working in the nursery ("I loved that").

— "Playing God," trying to speed up the slow therapy process with a man whose arm had been paralyzed by a stroke. ("I more or less hypnotized him," Bill said, "and when he tried, he moved his hand and started to cry, and I felt embarrassed and ashamed of myself for . . . playing my little game there.") Not that he had done the patient any harm, but Bill was bothered by the awareness that it was possible for him to play God.

— The white patient from the South whose left side had been paralyzed after being attacked by a hatchet. ("We had a great relationship, a white man from the South and a black man from the North. I don't know what his political views were, but we got along fine. And it wasn't that kind of relationship where I was a good boy or anything. When he wasn't right, I'd chew him out.")

— The patient with brain damage who would add numbers when he couldn't think of a word. ("You'd ask him, 'How you doin'?' and he'd say, 'Oh, five-six or 'twelve-four.' You'd start laughing; he'd start laughing. They were great times.")

Had he decided to make a career of physical therapy, "I think — I hope — I would have been a *great* physical therapist."

Physical therapy was one satisfying part of his Navy career. Athletics was another. For example, at Quantico Marine Base he made the track team, and achieved a height of 6'5" in the high jump.

But dissatisfaction was gnawing at him. In the service he met "a lot of guys I knew didn't have as much as I had upstairs — yet they were struggling to get an education. I realized finally that I was committing a sin, a mental sin. . . ."

There was more to it.

"I was getting older. I didn't particularly like the Navy. I didn't like the guys who were bossing me around, telling me to clean up any old thing any old time for no reason — 'Do it because I said to do it.' I knew I didn't want to stay in the service. Now the only way you can get out of it is to get yourself an education, unless you want to go back to civilian life and wait on tables, not wait on tables but just take glasses off and that kind of thing, which I knew was where I was headed."

It was a turning point in his life. He decided he'd like to become a teacher.

"With that awakening, I made a mad scramble — I forced myself to study, and started to develop pretty good habits."

He took a special high school equivalency exam — a type of IQ test — and won a General Education Diploma.

The next question was how to further his ambition of teaching, how to get into college, how to make it through four years with little money. Then it all seemed to fall into place. His interest in athletics, which had taken him away from his studies in the first place, was now the key. He decided to try for an athletic scholarship.

7

BILL AND RIGGY

A SHOT AT THE DEAN'S LIST

Ordinarily, when someone is trying to win a scholarship it's a pretty serious, businesslike occasion. Not so with Bill Cosby.

Bill was the only athlete Gavin White, assistant director of athletics at Temple University, Philadelphia, remembers interviewing for a scholarship who had him roaring with laughter for a whole day.

At a track meet at Villanova when Cosby was with his service team, he introduced himself to White, coach of the Temple track team, and said he was interested in attending Temple.

"What do you jump?" White asked him, and Cosby jokingly replied that he thought he could jump 7 feet (a height few jumpers can clear). White, in the same spirit, shot back, "Well, that's too good for Temple; we only jump 5'8"."

Then Bill told about the time in a National AAU com-

"If I had it to live over, I realize now that it is possible to be a good student *and* to chase that ball, and to have a lot of fun."

petitions when he had jumped from eight in the morning until three in the afternoon, finally clearing the bar at 6'5" (his best height). He got up from the pit, confident he'd won, only to find that the competing jumpers, who'd been sitting around in their sweatsuits, were only *starting* at 6'5" and raising the bar from there. "I said good-bye," Cosby commented, adding that he finished "about 84th" in that meet (actually 17th).

Cosby remembers that he "kind of took to Gavin right away," and the feeling was mutual.

Since Bill was well qualified — he had had his high school diploma and the papers to prove his athletic prowess, including the ability to high jump 6'5" — in short order he was granted a four-year track scholarship, on the condition that he keep up his grades.

So in September 1960, at the age of 23 — when most college students have already been graduated — Bill Cosby enrolled in Temple University's College of Education, feeling both groovy and frightened, majoring in physical education and looking to a career as a teacher.

Billy Rose of Ambler, Pennsylvania, himself a popular teacher and assistant track coach at Upper Dublin (Pennsylvania) High School, ran track and had some classes with Cosby at Temple. He remembers that Cos, as they used to call him, "was always helping somebody" with studies. Sometimes Cosby would imaginatively try to help himself. In anatomy class, for instance, when he couldn't think of the name of a particular muscle, he'd make one up, usually something like "latissifer," which was always good for a laugh if not a high mark. Still, he did well.

Though Cos was on the basketball, football, and track teams in his freshman year, leaving little time for books, he was a sharp student and almost made the dean's list, an honor reserved for students with high averages. "Physical education major or not, it's still groovy," Bill commented with understandable pride.

His big accomplishments, however, were in sports.

Seasoned by his Quantico experience, the powerfully built and fully developed athlete proved to be a versatile and valuable addition to the Temple Owls roster.

He made the freshman basketball team ("an acceptable player" was the summation of one teammate), he played freshman and varsity football, and, on the track team, he not only distinguished himself in high-jumping, but also broad jumped (long jumped), ran the low hurdles, threw the javelin and discus, and put the shot.

"I thought he was a tremendous athlete," White said. Though primarily a high jumper, Cos would be used in as many events as they thought him capable, and in one meet he scored in five different events.

According to White, Cosby trained hard as a track athlete. "When he first came here," the coach said, "he was not a runner so to speak, and yet he took on the rigorous training that was necessary to become a hurdler." When one young teammate got hurt, "Bill moved right in and had the job the rest of the year."

Serious as he was about succeeding as an athlete, Cos had plenty of light moments, whether he was singing "Our Boys Will Shine Tonight" on the bus, or running out, as the team lined up for javelin practice, shouting, "If you hit me, you win."

Once he used a combination of natural wit, imagination, and "conmanship" to do to his competitors what athletes politely refer to as "psyching."

It was the Mid-Atlantic meet, with some excellent high jumpers participating, including at least one man who had bested him earlier in the season by three or four inches.

Bill gathered his competitors around him and pointed to a slight lip of grass or dirt at the approach to the bar. "Don't come off the lip too hard because I saw a lot of guys slipping," he deadpanned. His opponents, taking his advice, changed their step whenever they approached the lip. As a result, even a fellow who had jumped 6'5" was unable to clear 6 feet, and Cosby managed to take the title with a jump of just 6 feet.

When he tells people he won the Middle Atlantic High Jump championship, he proudly adds, "of the world." A true statement, since there isn't another Middle Atlantic championship elsewhere.

As a runner, Bill was introduced to what trackmen affectionately call Rigor Mortis or Riggy (a sudden and painful tightening-up of the muscles).

When Cosby's group would be doing the 300-yard dash that ended practice sessions, Cos might be in the lead and suddenly pull up, shouting in mock agitation, "Oh, I can't go on, Riggy Mortis got me." Or he might announce proudly, "At no time did Riggy get on my back" — while lying flat on his back.

Onstage today, Cos tells how the coach drafted him into being a relay runner when the anchor man — the last to run and generally the swiftest on the relay squad — is sidelined by an injury. (In the routine about being cool, Cos already has begged an opponent to let him win the high jump so he can impress some girls in the stands.)

"Anchor man?" protests Cosby, who's already upset at having to be in the relays at all.

The coach is reassuring. He promises, "We'll open up such a big lead, you can just about walk around the track."

Happy with another chance to impress the girls, Cosby accepts. The first two men on the team do open up a big lead, but as the third teammate is about to pass Cos the baton, it hits his leg and then flies up into the air.

When finally he gets the baton, he is so proud at hearing his name over the public address system, he decides to give it all he's got. But as he comes down the stretch, old Riggy strikes. Cosby loses, and even the homely girl among the dozen he was trying to impress says, "Boy, you really look bad."

But in truth, as a trackman at Temple, Cosby looked awfully good. In White's words, Cosby "showed up real well right from the beginning." The freshman team was one of the best ever. Among his accomplishments in his sophomore year, Cosby was the Temple Owls' second-best scorer with $50^1/_2$ points, winning (or psyching out) the Middle Atlantic Conference University Division high jump championship, and finishing fourth in the Middle Atlantic Conference broad jump competition.

As a member of Temple's freshman football team, he was regarded as a fine blocker by White, who also coached that club. Cosby, weighing 190 pounds during football season (178 in track season), "could knock them dead," White said. "He just had a knack."

_____

Always funny primarily as a storyteller, Cos would entertain the other football players during the boring nights at training camp. He had a whole series of race anecdotes. (Sample: The first Negro elected President of the United States reporting to a friend, "Everything's fine, except there's a whole bunch of 'for sale' signs going up on Pennsylvania Avenue.")

He was quite serious about his athletics and training, but "didn't believe in all these old pep talks. I'd just as soon get out there and play."

He'll always remember one particular talk, which he heard as a member of the freshman gridiron squad. The team had been invited to play a special night benefit. It was freezing cold, there were few spectators in the stands, and the visibility was so bad some people were lighting matches to see. White remembers, "I got so angry, I gave a typical coach's pep talk. We'd show them we're not city hicks, they can't do this to us."

As White spoke, the players got more and more charged up, until they were angry enough to commit mayhem.

As it comes out in Cosby's routine, "The Pep Talk," the coach is yelling:

"Let me hear you say 'Kill,' "

"Kill," the players roar back.

"Let me hear you say 'Fight.' "

"Fight."

"Let me hear you say 'We want to win.' "

"We want to win."

"Are you ready?"

"Yeah, ready,"

"Go out and get 'em. . . ."

Just about frothing at the mouth, the team charges forward, but the door is locked (as it actually had been after White's talk).

He made White the butt of other stories, accusing him in one of calling a play that would run right over his mother in a wheelchair.

Yet the fact is he had a tremendous respect for White. "I enjoyed Gavin very much. I really looked up to him. A strong guy, in almost a religious sort of way. Never heard him say a swear word . . . A real human being . . . Sort of like a beautiful example of what a coach should be. A great sense of humor [but] you knew he meant business. Always studying, always looking for the best approach for a kid to get the best out of it."

Cosby wasn't happy, though, with the playing style of the varsity under coach George Makris. "I wasn't that great because I wasn't doing what I wanted," Cosby said. "They made me a fullback; I wanted to be a halfback. I wanted to catch passes; I was never given a chance to do that."

Cosby didn't always hide his feelings and sometimes would be openly critical.

One night the backs were running kickoff returns in practice. It was understood the man returning the kick would run right through the middle; the defending team, of course, knew where the ball-carrier would run and were set to cream him. But when it was Cos' turn, instead of running through the middle, he went to the outside. As Cosby's roommate Don Council recalls it, the coach demanded to know why and Bill replied that everybody knew what to anticipate. "I feel like a fool." The coach ordered him to take a lap around the field for his insubordination.

"You know," Cos reminisces now, "guys like to show off in practice."

"If you don't develop discipline you don't have a team," says Makris.

Makris said that Cosby, "an excellent trainer, always well conditioned," was a credit to the team and the university. He played him at fullback (second string) because he was bigger than most of the other backs.

Despite any displeasure he might have felt, Cosby gave his all on the field — his collar bone was broken in three places — and was at least once ejected from a game.

Cosby, Makris said, was "a fiery competitor, who wanted to excel." He played football "with drive and determination, the same qualities that made him such a good comedian." Makris, like others who know Cosby, considers him "a born comic" — he was funny all the time, even at normally tense pregame moments.

———————

Don Council, a Camden (N.J.) high school teacher and developer of a black history curriculum, was a sophomore and Cosby a freshman when they ran together. Next year as football teammates, they were assigned to be roommates when the team was on the road.

In Council's view, Cosby, an imposing six-footer,

At Temple, Cos played football and freshman basketball, starred in track and field and almost made the Dean's list. Below, left to right, he prepares to throw the discus and put the shot. The facing page shows Cos practicing with his javelin.

was a tremendous athlete, ideally built, tapering from broad shoulders to thin ankles. "Few people are tougher," said Council, an excellent athlete himself, recalling how Cos had knocked a Buffalo player's helmet off with one tackle, causing him to lose a shoe.

Cosby was tough in other ways. Always one to play pick-up basketball on the spur of the moment, Bill once got into a game with Don in a rough neighborhood. ("We shouldn't even have been there," Council said.) After Cosby had fouled a player, neighborhood toughs threatened the two outsiders, but, Council recalled, Cosby stood right up to them.

Once, Bob Cosby remembers, Bill was spat at, and proceeded to "deck" his uncouth assailant.

"That's one reason he doesn't go on marches," Bob said. "He might start swinging."

Bill got his first car while at Temple and began a hobby that's carried on through his success. One his family remembers as the Black Rat, an old Dodge he called Captain America (he does a routine about it). "I wrecked it," Bill remembers (his mother was billed for the bark of the tree he skidded into), and after that he just started buying cars — fast cars, slow cars, big cars, little cars. "I ran them all."

Cos got to be a sort of unofficial roommate of Council's at Temple itself as well as on the road. Since Cosby lived in Philadelphia his scholarship did not include room and board privileges, but because it was quite a trip between the university and his home, he'd often sleep in the dorm with Council. Sometimes he'd bring his drums to the room for a jam session (Bill worked a couple of times with a jazz group known as the "Philadelphians").

For meals at school he'd borrow someone's meal card, and after awhile he was seen so regularly on the chow line, he no longer had to show a card.

On the road, according to Council, Bill was a neat roommate. An orderly person and a take-charge guy, Cos would pick up candy and buy newspapers and tell Don to pick up the key on their way to the room and he'd make sure to have the hotel clerk call them in the morning so they'd be up on time. To Cos, said Council, "life had an order. He contemplated what he would do."

Bill was a friend of "just about everybody" on the football team, according to Council, and used to enjoy "sounding" — playfully exchanging cutting insults with his teammates.

Cos, whom somebody had dubbed "Bogart" for the dramatic way he played basketball, used to make up nicknames for his friends. He called Don "Jack Johnson-Jack Johnson" after the old fighter Council resembled when he shaved his head.

For amusement Cos would sometimes take something by Shakespeare — Hamlet, for instance, and give a comical reading of a somber section, or he might do a funny impersonation of a pastor giving a sermon.

Usually, Cosby would dress casually in khaki pants, the way most of the students did. But, Council said, if he had money he would buy fairly expensive suits (some had to be given away because they were the wrong size). Don thinks Bill bought some items to distinguish himself from other people.

"It never seemed that money was very important to him," Council said, "but he wanted people to know he was there at all times."

To Council, being around Cosby was an experience in itself. "He was 'together.' "

Others share that view.

"He's one of the few beautiful people I know," said Ron Miller, a Philadelphia newsman for WCAU-TV, Philadelphia, who met Cos at Temple and had him as a guest on WRTI radio station at the university.

Miller and others who knew him in the days at Temple remember Cosby not only as a genuinely funny fellow but also as a serious conversationalist people respected. While he could find humor in any situation, "He was funny when it was time to be funny, serious when it was time to be serious," Council said.

In bull sessions, according to Miller, Cos could "riff" on any subject, and would always be the dominant figure in a group. Billy Rose remembers Cos as "good for putting into words what many people thought. . . . Often he'd be serious and talk about things like race and religion . . . where it's at."

In school his natural comic outlook sometimes made serious comment. He told a lot of racial stories, some of which, in the opinion of Council and others, were even funnier than what he now does professionally. He was funny in ordinary conversations (even about the weather) and some of his professional routines are stories he told his friends in the good old Temple days. He tried out "a lot of great ones," said Al Shrier, Temple's director of sports information; often college friends would "bribe" Cos with a continuing stream of coffee to keep him talking.

Like many of the campus athletes, Bill was a favorite of coeds of different backgrounds — "quite a lover," in the words of one of his friends. Explaining why he had no steady, he would kiddingly say about himself, "Cos is beautiful. . . . All the women should have a chance to share Cos."

It was rare that Cos went out on a formal date; more likely, if he had to be somewhere, he'd invite a girl to come along. His concept of a good time, Miller said, was "being with somebody he liked."

Not the most studious of athletes, Bill somehow managed to develop his own theory of history—that events are shaped by the toss of a coin, the way football games are opened. On the Revolutionary War he speculates the Colonials won the toss and announced: "We want to wear any kind of clothes we feel like and shoot from behind rocks and trees, and the British have to wear red coats and walk in a straight line."

8

THE FUNNY BARTENDER

"CONSIDERABLE PROMISE"

A bar, a few printed paragraphs, and a substitute host on a TV show all contributed to changing Bill Cosby from a student who told stories to friends for laughs into a professional who told them to national audiences for money.

In Bill's sophomore year at Temple he took a part-time job "to supplement no income." A club in downtown Philadelphia hired him as a bartender (for $5 a night plus tips), but he spent as much time amusing customers with witty patter as he did serving them drinks. Then a job next door paid him $12.50 a night.

Bar patrons and friends had been encouraging him to put his entertainment talents to work, and when he saw a Negro comic tell dirty jokes and bad racial jokes, Bill decided he could do better. He sought advice from his cousin and good friend Del Shields, now executive secretary of the National Assocation of Television and Radio Announcers, who had a record show on WDAS-FM. With his help, Bill got booked into other small night clubs around Philadelphia, leaving some pretty forgettable ones behind.

Cos started out as a professional comedian as part of a write-it-yourself twosome, but he and the other funny fellow, Joe Johnson, Jr., worked together only about two weeks before his partner quit. The problem, according to Cosby, was "We'd get up there two minutes before it was time to go on and he'd say 'that stuff's not funny.' "

Cos would stay up late working on his act, listening to comedians he liked — Carl Reiner, Mel Brooks, Jonathan Winters, Lenny Bruce, Bob Newhart, Brother Dave Garner, and others — and memorizing comedy routines the way singers memorize songs. "It was all part of my conmanship." Very early in his career, he did sketches originated by Bob Newhart, Mel Brooks, and Mort Sahl, among others, but always gave credit to the comedian from whom he had "borrowed."

He'd "bounce" material off his brothers and friends, then try it on the paying customers, apparently with success. His reputation spread as far as New York and he was booked into the Gaslight Cafe, in the Greenwich Village section of the city, at $60 a week for five nights to fill in between two folksingers. Bill was given a room (without plumbing) to share over the club. He paid somebody $5 to use a shower. (When he was later booked into the Bitter End in the Village the room he had there *did* have plumbing.)

In April 1962, Cosby was given a 105-word write-up in a Temple Alumni Review article about students with interesting part-time jobs. The piece, accompanied by a full page picture of Cosby making a face, said he was earning "upwards of $16 a night to entertain in center city night clubs."

Among those who read the article were an alumnus and his fellow reviewer on *The New York Times,* who had done the first major interview-review piece on Dick Gregory. The idea was to do the same with Cosby.

But the *Times* wanted an exclusive story, so Albert R. Carlisle, director of Temple's office of public information, who was well aware of the importance of a story in the *Times* to Cosby and to the university, cautioned Bill to lie low and avoid talking to reporters from other papers.

"I did what he said," Cosby remembers. "I waited, I didn't talk to anybody."

Then finally on June 25, 1962, a review of Cosby's performance at the Gaslight Cafe appeared in *The New York Times,* across three columns with a picture of Cos — mugging.

"As an athlete," reviewer Paul Gardner wrote of Cosby, "he has already earned his first letter in track and football. As a cerebral comic, he is still on the second string, but several leading comics may have sleepless nights this fall.

"Although his output thus far is limited, his viewpoint is fresh, slightly ironic, and his best quips are extremely funny. He is a man of considerable promise...."

Of the review, Cosby admits, "I didn't even know what the value of the thing was." Yet the results were instantaneous. The review appeared on Monday, a traditionally slow day at clubs, but that night there was a long line to see Cosby.

Bill was held over at the Gaslight, his weekly salary upped, and offers began to come in from coffee houses and nightclubs across the country. His great ambition was to reach a point where he'd earn $300 a week for 10 years, then retire from show business to become a teacher.

It was around this time that one of the most important shapers of Cosby's career came into his life — Roy Silver, a onetime director of research for a chemical company, who had switched to managing entertainment talent. Today he is still Cosby's manager, a friend, and a partner with Cosby and Bruce Campbell in their own production company.

Silver (along with Fred Weintraub, his partner until Fred sold his interest) became Cosby's manager. The relationship was helped by the fact that "there was a great chemistry between Bill and Roy," according to Weintraub, owner of the Bitter End.

Every night Cos would do five or six shows, and Silver would take it all down on a tape recorder. Then the trio would go over the tapes, wondering aloud why one joke got a laugh and another didn't, or why the same piece of material got chuckles one show but not the next. They worked hard, line by line, sharpening here, cutting there, until they had a solid half-hour act.

9

A FUNNYMAN
WHO HAPPENS TO BE BLACK

A "FLOOD" OF HUMOR

At this point, most of Bill's stories were racial, and he was being touted as "another Dick Gregory," but Silver, Weintraub, and others had been telling him, in effect, to stop being a second Gregory and be the original Bill Cosby — get rid of the racial material.

Bill himself had had some doubts about doing racial things. Audiences, he said, are equally uncomfortable with color jokes and off-color jokes. It wasn't an easy choice, but "I decided instead of walking out telling everybody what color I was, I'd talk about the old neighborhood."

And so he began telling the kind of thing that "happened to me and, oddly enough, happened to a white kid in Pittsburgh or Atlanta as well as to a Negro kid in Harlem," the universality that has been the key to his popularity.

But following the advice of his manager meant des-

"I wanted to be a black buttoned-down comic, because I think
my people need it. They should see a different kind of comic,
with cool, dry humor, and I started out to do that."

On records and in night clubs, Bill told about his childhood. He recalls standing in the kindergarten schoolyard "with 27 snowsuits on" and wearing "idiot mittens with the string up your arm and around your neck. The only cool thing is you can talk to your left hand and listen with your right. . . . Find another kid with idiot mittens, pull his left mitten and he smacks himself in the face with the right!"

troying 80 per cent of the act they had worked so hard to perfect. Occasionally, in desperation, in the middle of performing he'd revert to his old routine about the first Negro president or other racial material, and this led to some tense moments between Silver and Bill, both strong-willed individuals. Yet they stuck with it and Cosby came up with a fresh new act.

One routine unveiled by Cosby, who would come to be known as the Negro comedian who *doesn't* use racial material, was Noah.

Cos has done more to popularize Noah than any-thing since the Old Testament account. In the comedy routine, as any Cosby fan knows, Noah is in his rec room sawing a piece of wood. (As always, he supplies his own sound effects, "Voopa, voopa, voopa.") Then a deep voice calls to him, "It's the Lord, Noah." A dumb smile appears on Noah's face. "Riiight," he says. "What do you want? I been good."

Told that the Lord wants him to build an ark, he says, "Riiight." Then, after a pause, "What's an ark?"

The Lord gives the dimensions — 300 cubits by 80 cubits by 40 cubits.

"Riiight," says Noah. "What's a cubit?"

"Let's see, a cubit . . ." Unable to define a cubit, the Lord announces, "I'm going to destroy all the people on the face of the earth. I am going to make it rain for a thousand days and a thousand nights."

"Just you and me, huh, Lord?" Noah pauses, then grins. "Hey, who is this really? . . Am I on *Candid Camera*?"

Receiving no answer, Noah suggests letting it rain for 40 days and 40 nights and "wait for the sewers to back up."

There is silence. Then the Lord answers, "Riiight."

As usual, Cosby plays all the parts, up to and including the Almighty, just as in other routines he plays Tonto (telling the Lone Ranger to get off his back); a tiger who lisps because he has only one sabertooth, a werewolf getting a haircut just as the full moon comes up ("a little more off the legs, kid").

Much of what Bill does isn't funny when someone tells you about it, but with his mobile, rubbery face, his expressive eyes, changing voice, and blowing and puffing his own sound effects into the mike, Cosby makes it hilarious.

One writer (Charles L. Mee, Jr., in *The New York Times Magazine*) said that Cosby performing "recalls the understated style of Bob Newhart, the characterizations of Jonathan Winters, and the sound effects of Victor Borge."

Cosby has always "written" his own material, though he doesn't put it down on paper. Friends at Temple say Cos used to do Noah there. Bill says he wrote it in the Cafe Wha', in Greenwich Village, where he'd try his routines out each day on the audience, not on his friends because "that would be cheating."

Noah had everybody saying "Riiight" and Cosby had club owners starting to notice him.

One of the places that hired Cos was the Gate of Horn in Chicago, where he did three weeks in the summer of 1962 for $250 a week. (The Gate of Horn had offered to give him two years' tuition at the University of Chicago and pay him $30 a week if he'd stay and play, but he decided to go back to Temple.)

Suddenly that summer he realized he was due in three days for Temple's preseason football drills. He reported out of condition and almost 15 pounds under-weight from working nights and eating only twice a day. Later in the season he had an offer to play Phil-adelphia's Town Hall for $250 and asked permission to fly out to meet the team in Toledo, but the athletic director turned him down. At a crossroad, Bill took the booking.

Though some have doubts that Bill was a good enough football player to rate a pro offer, Emlen Tun-nell was interested in getting Cos a tryout with the New York Giants football team. "But at that time," Bill said, "I'd started working in the coffeehouses and I was already making about a hundred dollars a week and I wasn't interested in getting run over."

With offers to perform gradually building, Bill had been torn by conflicting ambitions. He realized he couldn't do justice to comedy, football, and grades at the same time, so he decided to leave school. "Nobody wanted him to go," Billy Rose said, but Cos felt the time was ripe, there might not be a demand for his humor two years later.

So, in November 1962, for the second time in his life (the third, if you include his leaving Central High), Cosby became a dropout.

Carlisle and Shrier told Cosby, who fast became Temple's best known dropout, to keep in touch, and he took them at their word — calling collect from distant points to state, without any opening pleasantries, his business needs (say, Temple shirts for publicity pic-tures) and then to chat amiably for half an hour.

"I remember the celebration in this office," Carlisle said, "when Bill called from Seattle and the call wasn't collect. We knew he'd made it."

10
BILL AND COO

ENTER ROMANCE

Things were starting to move now for Cos.

In New York he was enjoying the Village scene, performing his act, and being a part of all that was happening, digging jazz, playing the drums, enjoying his car, talking with the groovy people who populated the scene.

In and out of New York, the naturally funny Philadelphian was more and more in demand as a performer, and at better pay.

While Bill was working at the Shadows in Washington, D.C., a friend arranged a blind date for him with a lovely looking University of Maryland psychology major, Camille Hanks, planting Bill in a bowling alley where Camille was struggling for strikes. Cos needled her about her game and laughed at her, but soon she was laughing at him.

They took to each other immediately. Though she

hadn't been interested in dating an entertainer, Camille liked the brash, self-assured young man. She was impressed with his sincerity and humor, and, when she saw his show at The Shadow's, his talent.

"The first time I saw her, I said I'm going to marry her," Bill said. "I just liked her. She was corny, straight ahead, you know. I said I'll take her and mold her," he laughed.

As to what she saw in him, he said, "I don't know. I blew a lot of smoke around her. She couldn't see anything."

Camille's parents, however, did see something, something they didn't like. Her father, Guy Hanks, a chemist at Walter Reed Hospital, and her mother, who operated a nursery, didn't want their daughter to marry an entertainer, especially a dropout with an uncertain future.

They went so far as to send her off to live with relatives in Virginia, in order to keep the couple apart.

Bill, who by now had been booked again into the Bitter End, kept driving back and forth from New York to Maryland for their dates. He'd finish at the club at four in the morning, sleep till nine, drive nearly 200 miles to Maryland, take Camille for a hamburger and a movie (he often dozed off), kiss her good-bye, and, fighting sleep, drive back to New York.

It took him only four or five dates to be sure Camille was the girl for him, and in case his longdistance commuting to be with her didn't prove he "really dug her," he decided he'd have to show her he "really, really cared." So Bill had a friend in Greenwich Village make an engagement ring — "It had pieces of black specks in the stone" — for $400!

Camille accepted the expensive ring. But her parents were worried about the insecurity of marriage to an entertainer, and they strenuously objected. Mr. Hanks wanted Bill to go back to college; Mrs. Hanks just didn't care for her daughter's suitor. They sent Camille to Virginia to think things over, and for awhile she did seem to have a change of heart. There was even a good-bye note.

Then, he continued, he came back into town. "I put the freeze on her. Didn't call or nothing." He lowered his voice, saying, "She came begging." He laughed aloud.

When Bill and Camille were reunited, he said they'd have to get married or stop seeing each other for good, and Camille agreed. This time, Bill asked Camille's father for her hand, and he reluctantly consented. On January 25, 1964, they were married in Olney, Maryland, about three miles from the Hanks' home.

Someone said Bill and Camille were married on a basketball court that had been converted into a church. Bill is enough of a sports lover to have said "I Do" in that kind of setting, but the truth is the ceremony took place behind the church because Camille is Catholic and he isn't.

The newlyweds went to New York for their honeymoon, with Bill spending most of his wedding night on stage at Basin Street East, a club across from their hotel. Bill said, "Camille sat up in the middle of the night and asked me where she was and what she was doing there."

Camille adjusted to marriage, and Bill, who'd been a bachelor 26 and a half years, did too — despite his claim that he nearly fractured his skull from walking into nylon stockings hanging in the bathroom. He jokes about having to report in, punch the clock, and give her the money, but he also says of Camille, "Physically, she is beautiful; inside, she's got them all beat."

While Bill was courting Camille, he and his manager were wooing television, with little success. As well as Bill was doing, Roy Silver was convinced that Cos needed a crack at a national TV audience to skyrocket into the entertainment big leagues. He even had items planted in newspaper columns to give the impression that Bill was being considered for various TV series, but this was more wishful press agentry than fact.

Bill had been mentioned a few times for possible guest shots on NBC's big-audience *Tonight* show, but no one was taking chances on the relative unknown. Then Johnny Carson took some time off as m.c. of the show, and Allan Sherman, the funny folksinger, who happened to know Silver, filled in.

Cosby got to perform his routine for the producer, and then for him and Allan Sherman together. The producer was lukewarm, but Allan said, "Good, let him on."

On the show, Cos did his karate bit. ("There must be 23 million karate schools in Greenwich Village alone. I imagine this is because after you've been graduated from a karate school, there is no better feeling than knowing you can wipe out your whole neighborhood.")

Cos was a smash. He was invited back to the *Tonight* show whenever he was in town. He's since appeared many, many times and even hosted several stanzas. Firmly established as a $1500-a-week performer, he got offers to appear at leading night clubs, in one-man concerts, and on other TV shows — *Hootenanny, Ed Sullivan, Gary Moore, Andy Williams, Jack Paar.*

By now, he had such credits as the hungry i in San Francisco (he reportedly was the first comedian to be held over there); The Flamingo in Las Vegas; Harrah's at Lake Tahoe; and Mr. Kelly's in Chicago. (His opening there was possibly the only time he's ever experienced stage fright — "I did a bad show then," he admits, "but that was my first time going into a big room." Next show, he did fine.)

And besides playing the more sophisticated nightclubs, he was now branching out in still another direction — records.

Allan Sherman introduced him to Warner Bros.-Seven Arts, where he signed a recording contract and went on to become one of the best-selling LP comedy recording artists of all times. As of late 1968, he had done six comedy record albums and two song albums, plus a couple of singles, and he has a new comedy album planned for spring 1969.

For a couple of months, his first four albums were in the top 50 best-selling charts at the same time.

In October 1963, he recorded *Bill Cosby is a Very Funny Fellow RIGHT!* live at the Bitter End. Sherman, who coproduced that and other Cosby records, wrote on the album, "Bill Cosby has a wonderful, cock-eyed fresh sense of humor. He is so good that what he has is more than talent; he has the gift of comedy. He has something that makes you feel delight when you're with him. . . . in an office, in a nightclub, or standing on a street corner. He has joy in being alive and he communicates it to you, so that when you're with him, you too are glad you're alive."

11

THE SPY'S THE LIMIT

A RHODES SCHOLAR NO LESS

A youngster once asked Bill Cosby where he got his glasses and he replied, "They issue them whenever you become a spy."

He was referring, of course, to the hip, educated espionage agent he played for three years on NBC's *I Spy* series, a role that catapulted him to greater fame and made him familiar to a larger regular audience than he had ever enjoyed.

On the program, the real-life school dropout portrayed a Rhodes scholar able to speak seven languages. The character, Alexander Scott, poses as trainer and companion to a fellow U.S. intelligence agent masquerading as a top amateur tennis player.

But what was significant about it was not the nature of the part, but the color of the man who played it. Bill Cosby — who shunned racial material in his act — became the first Negro to costar in a continuing network series.

Before signing Bill to *I Spy*, producer Sheldon Leonard checked into Cosby the person. "From every source," Leonard told *TV Guide*, "I learned Bill Cosby was a tireless worker, a man striving to do his best."

The man responsible was Sheldon Leonard, a former movie actor turned successful TV producer, who had seen Cos doing his karate routine on a variety show and liked the way he looked and performed. He was impressed by Bill's physical power, agility, sense of humor, and "capacity for warmth." Though he hadn't envisioned a black man for the role, he thought Cosby would be ideal in the part of sidekick to series' star Robert Culp, and decided to pursue the idea. He went about convincing network and advertising agency people of the merits of the idea. There was some concern that bigoted stations might not take the show with a colored costar, but the green light was given.

Bill's first reaction was that it wasn't going to happen — "it's too good to be true."

But then he had his doubts.

Except for his comedy routines or his performances in school shows, Bill had never acted before. "I was frightened," he recently confided to an interviewer for *Kaleidoscope* on San Francisco's KQED, "not necessarily for my people; I was frightened for Bill Cosby."

Yet, at the beginning he had told a newspaperman, "If it fails, I hope it's because I, as an actor, did not come off well. I hope, if it does fail, they won't say we'll never try this again with a Negro. I hope it's a case of Cosby did not come off, not a Negro did not come off."

As a successful nightclub comedian venturing into unfamiliar territory, he knew he'd be taking a big gamble. But, he said, "TV is the field that develops heavy hitters. Let's see if I can qualify."

Then, too, though Cosby is a firm believer that "a man should be judged for himself regardless of his color," there was the opportunity of pioneering a major breakthrough for Negroes in television.

Another thing that appealed to him was the fact that Alexander Scott was definitely "not a Tonto," not an obedient man-of-one-syllable serving his master.

Glad that Scott "wears a tie, has brains, and shows the Negro being himself, a human being," Bill cast aside his initial reluctance and decided to say yes to the chance to play "the first Negro champion on TV."

The signing of Cosby caused considerable excitement throughout the television industry. The show, one of the most expensive in TV history, would shoot its adventures "on location" at the actual, often exotic, locales where episodes were set. By the time *I Spy* had its premiere, more than 180 stations affiliated with NBC had agreed to carry it, and this figure would later climb, with less than a handful holding out.

But all wasn't under control, as far as Bill was concerned. Bill was still worried, not only about possible failure, but that the show might "receive artificial praise for the wrong reason. . . . I'd like *I Spy* to be judged on its entertainment values."

At first, Cosby's doubts about his acting capabilities seemed well founded. His acting was "terrible," he said. "Just what it was supposed to be. Awful."

At the beginning, "he mumbled everything," said Leonard. "He didn't listen to other people's lines, so he didn't react properly."

Cosby agrees. During the filming of the pilot in Hong Kong, Bill found that the hardest thing was learning to listen. He memorized Culp's last word, and would come in when he heard it, without listening to anything else. "That is not acting."

At ease doing comedy monologues before thousands of people, he was tight and wooden doing dramatic scenes in front of the director and technicians, and couldn't wait to get the words out. "I would either say my lines without moving my face, or move my face and forget my lines." And he had to learn how to get his laughs as an actor rather than as a comedian.

A drama coach was hired to give Cos a hand, but the one who helped most was Culp — not so much what he told Cosby as "the little pat on the back, the punch on the arm, you know, that kind of thing. And it helps a lot."

The day after the first program appeared in September 1965, Jack Gould, the television critic of *The New York Times*, wrote:

"Mr. Cosby . . . effortlessly demonstrated that he could develop into a promising actor."

Most of the credit for the fact that Cosby did develop belongs to his costar, who, Cos says, "is probably the greatest human being on this earth."

Cosby jokes that he met Culp at the USO. ("He was the only one who would dance with me.") Actually, they met on the set.

It wasn't a hit-it-off-right-away kind of thing, Cosby said. Their relationship just grew — "without trying, without getting in anybody's way."

Culp had reservations about Cosby's acting abilities when he first heard he'd costar. Culp helped him, Cos said, not only with his technical skill but with his acceptance of Cosby as a person. "He could make mincemeat out of me if he felt like it," Cosby said at the time, "but he's been very unselfish and a tremendous help."

They found they were, in Culp's words, "on the same wave length."

"We're closer than brothers," Cosby once said.

"We dig each other," said Culp. "I just love that guy."

Culp shifted some of the good lines to Cosby. He wrote several of the *I Spy* scripts and saw to it that Cosby's part was fatter. Gradually, Cosby moved up from costar in name to costar in fact, and it wasn't long before it was felt their parts were interchangeable. The hip, wry comic exchanges between the two came to overshadow the plot.

Rick DuBrow, a critic for United Press International, called the two "a very high-class comedy team — funny fellows with a genuinely contemporary flair."

In Hong Kong, Cosby found it difficult to get used to a rickshaw. "I didn't dig it," he said, referring to the idea of another human being pulling him around the city. Something else bothered him, too. In one scene, a little Chinese child rubs his face to see if his color would come off. "If anyone else rubs my face," Cos said afterward, "I'm going to rub back."

Needless to say, that sort of occurrence didn't come up in future *I Spy* scripts. In fact, there was hardly any reference to race at all in the three years the network show ran (independent stations now show reruns).

There were no race jokes in the scripts. Said Cos, "Even in real life, race jokes would be embarrassing to Bobby and to me."

The object was not to make any "statement" about race relations, Culp said, adding, "We did it with such success that finally people forgot he was black and I was white."

Apparently, they succeeded — though not without some hitches. A few Negroes complained that Cosby's role was little more than a new kind of stereotype. And there were some taboos imposed on the character Cosby played that didn't apply to the one portrayed by Culp. Kelly Robinson had his share of girls, for instance, but not Scotty. People began to think there was something wrong. "We got an awful lot of letters from other fellas who kind of dug us," Cosby said jokingly. He convinced his producer that he, too, should have girls, and a few times there was a romantic interest written into the script. And Cosby worked hard to get other Negroes roles on the show.

Perhaps most important, the *I Spy* heroes were seen week after week living, eating, working, and fighting together as equals, who, as Culp was quoted as saying, "don't know the difference between a colored and a white man. That's doing more than 100 marches. We're showing what it could be like if there had been no hate."

Cosby's acting kept improving — he was more relaxed and able to contribute a solid performance.

His new exposure as an actor before a vast TV audience helped his comedy career. The comedian who once dreamed of making $300 a week was earning $25,000 a week (and it would later be twice that amount and more). His record sales tripled. And his personal appearances at colleges and concert halls drew packed houses.

Riding high, he was invited to cohost the Emmy award ceremonies sponsored by the National Academy of Television Arts and Sciences and, more significantly, the comedian was nominated — as was Culp and others — for an Emmy for outstanding continued performance by an actor in a dramatic series.

In white tie and tails, Cosby served as master of ceremonies for the New York portion of the awards at the Americana Hotel. Then came the news that the winner in the best acting category was none other than Bill Cosby.

In a sense the award was the television industry's way of congratulating itself and though grateful for the honor, Cosby conceded that his Emmy had gone to a sentimental favorite — the first Negro costar in a TV series.

Cosby's tribute to Culp ("He lost this because he helped me") was heartwarming. More than one observer commented on the ironic fact that the novice had beaten out his teacher for the coveted award, but Cosby denies it was a touchy thing between them. "Bobby [Culp], being the great guy and the intelligent human being that he is, man, just said, 'Hey listen, let's go to work.' "

The next year, Cosby, a much improved actor, won again, and he made it three out of the three the year after that. He was surprised to win the first Emmy and the last one "more than anything." He feels he deserved the second one most, "But — I'll put some of the moments I have in television each year against any guy who's up for an Emmy. I managed some really good moments."

One of his good moments came in May 1968, when

he came to the podium to accept his third Emmy. He told how the series had shown, without fantasy, what should be — "and how groovy it would be" — a black man and a white man living together as harmonious human beings. He urged that TV do more "to show the racists and bigots they don't count."

Meanwhile, Cosby was amassing such other honors as a Golden Apple as most cooperative actor; a citation from The American Cinema Editors as best television actor; Temple's very first Order of the Owl award at its annual Founder's Dinner.

Four times he won Grammy awards for best comedy albums. *I Started Out as a Child, Revenge, What is Air?* and *Wonderfulness* won the awards from the National Academy of Recording Arts and Sciences, after his first one, *Bill Cosby is a Very Funny Fellow, Right!* was nominated but not elected.

And while all these honors were coming in, there was a special one that cast him in a new role entirely — fatherhood.

Where appropriate, stunt men were used for Cosby and Culp, not because they feared getting hurt but because of how the series would be affected if either star were injured.

"What can young people, black and white, do to help improve relations? They can try to be as fair with each other as humanly possible. And that's the important thing: fair. Not what *they* think is fair, but what *is* fair."

A scene (left); from an *I Spy* episode which gave Cosby a romantic interest. In an album Cosby tells of a girl he liked in college, "a philosophy major with an IQ of about 300,000," who went around asking questions like "Why is there air?" Says Cosby, any physical education major knows the answer —"air is to blow up volleyballs, to blow up basketballs".

In Hong Kong, the script had Bill falling down with his face next to a pigsty before shooting the villain. Cosby had to do the scene five times because the Chinese actor playing the villain wasn't able to "die" convincingly. He believed that the cameras capture the soul and that his pretended death might come true!

I Spy took Cosby to various parts of the world, and he reportedly worked with a tape recorder to master bits of languages that would come in handy on and off camera. He had Mexicans laughing when he patted a crew member's big stomach and said "*sandia,*" the Spanish word for watermelon.

Carl Reiner, the writer-comedian-producer, broke the news to Cosby that he'd been picked for *I Spy*. On the way to visit his wife who was ill in the hospital, Reiner stopped in to say Sheldon Leonard wanted to see Cos about a series.

"If I died tomorrow, I'd like people to think of me as a man who had a lot of potential and who never got to use all of it."

Where does Cosby get his new material from? "My wife, my kids, my family, myself," he answers. "There's enough humor right here." One of his warmly funny routines involves his impersonations of his two infant daughters and what they expect of their parents.

12

A NEW ROLE

"DADDY" COS

Bill and Camille ("She's the best present I ever had") had moved into the Cosby home in North Philadelphia. ("There's always room for one more," he had joked. "Someone will just have to slide over or get bumped out of bed.")

Then, with *I Spy* in the works, they moved to the West Coast. As Cos worked to get ready for the show's debut, he and his wife awaited another kind of premiere — the birth of their first baby.

Bill was rooting enthusiastically for a boy. In fact, he was so sure the baby would be the first of many boys, he had the following ad prepared for *Variety* (the weekly newspaper that show business people refer to as their "Bible"):

"I got the first man for my softball team."

He was in Hong Kong making the pilot of *I Spy* when on April 8, 1965, the news finally came: "A girl . . . and all's well."

The copy of the *Variety* ad was changed to:

"Oops." And then, "We'll treat her as if she was our own."

In the same vein, Shrier tells of the comic exchange Bill used to have when someone asked him, "How's the baby?"

"She's got a big L on her forehead," Cos would reply.

"What's the big L for?"

"Loser."

With all his kidding and despite any disappointment he may have felt over the fact that his baby was a future homemaker and not a home run hitter, Bill has been a loving father.

He told one interviewer in 1966 that the greatest experience in his life was "hearing about the birth of my daughter and getting to see her for the first time."

"As a father, he's a very gentle man," Camille was quoted by one magazine. "He's just crazy about the baby and so patient. He loves to bathe her and feed her and dress her. He's just a very loving father. As a husband, he has the same qualities."

Asked recently whether he still bathes and dresses her, Bill replied:

"Not too much. I used to. Now, I have a housekeeper who does it all. I've never been in favor of changing diapers; I don't like surprises."

Before his first child was born, Cos joked: "Haven't decided on the baby's name yet. Just gonna send him out to play and whatever the kids call him, that's his name."

Him, of course, turned out to be a *her*, and instead of leaving it up to the kids in the street, Camille named the baby Erika Ranee.

When possible, Camille and the baby traveled with Bill on his *I Spy* adventures in different parts of the U.S. and the world.

Then, the following year, Camille was expecting again, and Bill determined to be around when this baby was born.

He was about to board a plane for Denver to do a show when Camille went into labor, and he raced to the hospital in time to hear the baby's first howls. As he tells it: "I cancelled the flight, watched the baby, got on a Lear jet, arrived 10 minutes before show time — promoter was throwin' up — did the show, flew back . . . with a pink button, 'Another Loser.' "

The new baby, born three weeks early on July 23, 1966, is named Erinn Chalene.

Bill, still anxious to have a son, suspects he'll have to be "a little more militant about it." It's reported the Cosby's are expecting a third child early in 1969.

Despite his fantastically busy schedule, Cosby manages to spend time with his little girls. What do they do? "Oh, we go riding, swimming — we can't play basketball — we go out and chase squirrels in the park."

You would think that Bill, remembering how important and scarce gifts were in his own childhood, would tend to spoil his children. But when he was asked whether he buys them a lot of gifts, he said, "My wife does. I don't believe in it. If it were all left up to me, I'd get them like one present for Christmas. They're still too young to know what it's all about. Spend $900 for each kid, then they go down and play with the boxes."

He does what he can to protect his family's privacy;

"You can't be snotty and snobbish to your parents. Some parents are out of line, true. But I think if kids learn to be kind of cool about it, and think about these things, there's a certain way you can discuss things with your parents."

gracefully sidestepping people who want to interview or photograph his wife, although he has once in a while overruled Camille's aversion to photographers, because, he said, "I think it's important to have pictures of a Negro family with Momma and Poppa around, living in decent surroundings."

The surroundings are decent, all right. The Cosbys live in a rambling Spanish-style house in fashionable Beverly Hills. Complete with pool and the Sauna bath he got from Camille as a gift, the 16-room house is a far cry from the crowded three-to-a-bed apartments he grew up in in North Philadelphia. The house is the third the Cosbys have had since moving to the West Coast.

"I'm one of the lucky ones," Bill once said of his rise from the ghetto. "But I don't intend to rely on luck; that's why I'm out there, hustling as hard as I am."

His hustle has reaped big dividends. For a single week in Las Vegas, Cos now earns $50,000; in September 1968, he reportedly was paid $17,000 for just one performance in Saratoga, New York.

He's one of three partners in a company producing records, movies, and TV shows, some of which will star Cosby. He's starring in an NBC series of entertainment specials; played a key role in a CBS series on the Negro contribution to America; and had a million dollar, five-day-a-week five-minute comedy series on top radio stations throughout the country.

Bill once told an interviewer:

"Financially I'm a big success, I guess, but I realize that money doesn't really matter. It's the dignity I'm working for."

No one disputes the dignity part. But, at the same time, an associate says, Bill has no guilt complex about his success — "he's happy he's rich."

Cosby acknowledges his yearly income is over a million dollars (some put it in the millions), but complains he gets to keep "maybe one-hundredth" of it (an exaggeration, though taxes are high, possibly 90 cents of every dollar goes to Uncle Sam).

Was making a lot of money a big drive for the fellow who grew up with very little money?

"Sure," he said. "Sure it was. All those things, the big house, the car, everything. Just a matter of bobbing and weaving until you're comfortable with it."

He even bought himself a diamond ring. "I took it off because I felt funny with it. But at least I had it."

He's bought his wife so many mink and other fur coats "we could start our own store." As to clothing for himself, he dismisses the subject with, "No, I'm pretty cool. Six, seven, suits every once in a while, that's about it."

13

THE PROUDEST MOMENTS

THE HAPPY TIMES

Perhaps most important to Bill, his spiralling success has enabled him to achieve what he considers one of the proudest moments of his life — "Being able to walk into my home and say to my mother that 'you will not scrub any more floors or work in anybody else's house' . . . being able to give her not only the love that I have for her, but also take care of the finer things." The one time shoeshine boy who had promised his mother he'd give her everything she hadn't had has given her a mink stole, two mink coats, and a car for Christmas.

His brothers have profited from Bill's success, too. When Bob went to register for classes at Delaware State, concerned about paying, he found that his tuition had already been taken care of by Bill.

"When you become momentarily wealthy, you look back on your family and you want to do for the mother

and the father especially," Bill said. "Well, I was will-
ing to buy my mother a 50- or 60-thousand-dollar
house and put a maid and butler in there, but, unde-
manding, she rejected that. She said, 'Just fix up the
house I live in now, because all my friends are here.'"

And so Bill did fix up the attached house on North
21st Street in Philadelphia. He took care of remaining
payments on it, and now the white stucco structure,
with black trim and awnings, belongs to the Cosbys.

At Bill's Beverly Hills home, he has a staff of two —
"a wonderful cook and his wife."

He did have a chauffeur, but let him go. "It was no
fun sitting in the back."

Cosby continues to indulge his fondness for cars.
He'll tell an audience he has a chauffeur follow him
around in a Rolls-Royce while he walks along and
points it out or waits for someone to say: "Wow, look
at that car."

"It's mine."

"No kidding."

Actually he did own a '37 Rolls, had it fixed up, but
didn't like it ("I figured maybe for $24,000 the place I
was going to would come to me") and donated it to
Studio Watts where it was raffled off.

"If you're wealthy, you turn idiot and buy a $17,000
Ferrari," he told one television audience. He does own
a maroon Ferrari and a Rover.

He's been known to slip out in the early hours of
the morning and drive at 120 miles an hour along a
deserted road, to get rid of his emotions.

"Well, I think everybody does — all of the stars.
It's kind of like getting away from everybody," he said.
"I don't punish the car. I just get in the car and take

my daughter or somebody and we just go for a little spin. There's nobody around. It's just kind of a way to get away from it all."

Often, of course, he prefers to get into the thick of it all, instead. Las Vegas is a favorite recreation spot for Cosby, and he's been known to win and lose hundreds of dollars at the gambling tables. More often Vegas means a chance for Cos to listen to jazz ("my first or second great night club love") or being pulled up on the stage of one of the posh clubs to join in a song, joke-telling, and jam sessions with a host of other celebrities.

In the entertainment world, too, he seems to be getting even more deeply involved, expanding his interests.

In the summer of 1967, the high priced star worked at the minimum union scale ($28.33 a night) at Los Angeles' Whiskey a Go Go. Supported by a group called the "Watts 103rd Street Rhythm Band," Cosby the comedian-actor became Silver Throat the singer. He's recorded two song albums, *Silver-throat* (one number on it, "Little Old Man," rose to number three among pop singles), and later *Hooray for the Salvation Army Band*. Why the new career? "I like the music — not necessarily my voice, but the music."

"Little Old Man," was one of the numbers Cos did in his NBC entertainment special March 18, 1968. (Two more Bill Cosby specials are due to follow.)

In the first one, the emphasis was on his youth in Philadelphia, where he played football with Fat Albert and Weird Harold and all the rest, and lost his tonsils. He stood in Philadelphia at the spot where he'd been hit by a slush ball (he still misses snow), got into a

"I like what I'm doing and I don't think it's necessary to have a drink. Why do people drink? To relax. Well, if you're already relaxed, how much more do you want?"

game of touch football, and reminisced about a favorite breakfast: orange soda and a cupcake.

The program was a production of Campbell-Silver-Cosby Corp., the company formed to handle all his activities plus those of others. They've contracted to do five pictures for Warner Bros.—Seven Arts, the first of which is *The Picasso Summer*. The second is *God Save the Mark*, a murder-comedy-mystery which stars Cos as "the mark," the too trusting fellow who is taken advantage of by everyone.

CSC has formed a record company, known as Tetragrammaton, and it's a good bet that Cos' next comedy record, due about March 1969, will be on that label.

In the summer of 1968 Bill completed seven months of recording five-minute radio comedy shows for Coca Cola, presented five days a week on the top-40 stations in some 500 cities. A favorite character on the show, (in which Frank Buxton, the producer, appeared with Cosby), was the Brown Hornet, who fights crime in a car called "The White Beauty" and lives in a Harlem walkup and doesn't have a telephone.

Bill has signed to do an hour-long special every year for the next five on NBC, as well as two animated cartoon specials and several other shows. The cartoon specials, with music by Miles Davis, will be based on Bill's childhood and feature such pals as Weird and Fat.

Beginning in the fall of 1969, Bill will star on NBC in a weekly prime time, half-hour comedy-adventure series about a San Francisco Bay area schoolteacher and his family.

When asked about the situation comedy he's always talked of, where he and his family would live next to somebody like the Jack Lemmons, he'd commented, "We'll get one going. That'll be it. That'll be the sign-off. That'll be my swansong."

"You just get a chance to
show off and let your friends
see exactly what it's like
—and they get to share what
you have."

14

COS AND THE CAUSE

CONTRIBUTING THE GROOVY WAY

Cosby once said he went into show business to make money, not to lead a march. He respects Dick Gregory and his genuine commitment to civil rights, yet this is not his style.

He feels that individuals like Gregory and the late Dr. Martin Luther King, and such Negro groups as the Deacons and the Muslims "do their jobs in their own way. My way is to show white people that Negroes are human beings with the same aspirations and abilities that whites have."

Bill, whom a friend describes as militant though softspoken, is tired of those who say he's not doing enough in the rights movement. In a reference to pressure exerted on people in the public eye, he said: "You know, you could be shooting pool in North Philadelphia or in Watts, and the minute you become a great pool shooter, along comes a guy and says, 'What have you done for civil rights?' "

Sammy Davis, Jr., was quoted as saying:

"Bill Cosby carries as much weight on his shoulders as any Negro I know, and he wears it as well and as lightly as any man could. He may not be a frontrunner in the cause — that's not his nature — but he's totally committed. He gives freely of his time and money. In Watts, he's worked hard for community theatre. The cats on the corner dig him, and he represents something very important to me."

Cosby has participated in such demonstrations as Solidarity Day in the Poor People's March in June 1968, where he acted as an informal opening master of ceremonies.

"Sure," he said, "I've done quite a few things. But you don't want to say to someone, 'here's a list of things I've done.' " Actually Cosby is deliberately close-mouthed about his service in civil rights and other causes. What he's done and for whom is something he wants to keep for himself. He'd be "awfully embarrassed, self-conscious" to reveal it, even in a general way.

He said, "If I help any black people or black group, it's because I want to help. And I do — in my own way. Not for the benefit of Bill Cosby; publicity is zero on this. I lay out a certain number of dollars, but I don't want anybody talking about it." (His public relations man, Joe Sutton, confirms that Cosby won't let him publicize his contributions.)

One professional contribution he's made that is known to the public was his participation in the first two segments of the seven-part CBS series, *Of Black America.*

"I think of all the times I've showed up for a march

or a parade, or I've given to an organization, to me that show was the most powerful of all the things you could give."

The first program called *Black History — Lost, Stolen, or Strayed,* traced the Negro's contributions to science, invention, medicine, exploration, and the winning of the west and included a history of the stereotyped ways the Negro has been portrayed in movies.

"You don't read in history books about the four black regiments with Teddy Roosevelt when he charged up San Juan Hill, or about the 38,000 black Union soldiers who died in the Civil War," Cosby said.

"When you take the way black history got lost, stolen, or strayed . . . when you think about those kids drawing themselves without faces . . . when you remember the fine actors who had to play baboons to make a buck . . . I guess you gotta give us the sin of pride."

Cosby called *Of Black America* a "grand, great occasion, perhaps a once-in-a-lifetime kind of thing . . . and I was very, very proud to be a part of it. Very seldom do you get a chance to educate in a way that people will listen."

He intends to keep making his contribution to civil rights "the groovy way, the way *I* like to do it." This means no return to racial material in his act. As he once explained, his humor comes from the way he looks at things as a man, and the white person who listens to his act sees things the same way. "This must mean that we are alike. Right? So I figure this way I'm doing as much for good race relations as the next guy."

Cosby, who said he wants to be "a universally funny guy," hasn't changed his opinion that if his material is without race consciousness, he can actually do more to promote understanding.

When Cos started letting his hair grow "natural" Afro style, and grew a Rap Brown-style mustache, some people started thinking he had changed his approach.

Cosby discounts this, "People tend to get upset over things that are very, very silly . . . wanting to know, 'What you got that on for? What are you putting this on for?'

"The mustache doesn't make a guy any different, or what you wear. It doesn't make any difference."

Cos looks happy here (left) but "when too many people start to come at me for the autographs it makes the hair kind of stand up to hear them say: 'There he is; go get it.' I don't know what that represents. It's as if you're some kind of animal or something other than a human being."

About race relations in the entertainment world: "Things are getting better but those who seem to be taking a step, the token step, know and we know that that isn't the ultimate and that's why we have to keep pushing."

"I wish I could have gotten
the diploma and everything
first and still have what I
have today. That I would like.
That's something
I really want."

"You look a lot like Bill Cosby," a barber once told Cos. "Does he come here often?" Cosby asked. "Naw. They get their haircuts at those 20-dollar places."

15

COS THEN, COS NOW

TOADS AND T-SHIRTS

"Sweet William, how are you?"

Billy Rose, out on a blind date, looked around to see who was calling him. The amiable Ambler school-teacher, who was Cosby's classmate and track team-mate at Temple, had taken a girl he was eager to impress to Small's Paradise, a nightclub in New York's Harlem.

The familiar voice belonged to none other than Bill Cosby, who was there to help Sidney Poitier celebrate his birthday. In a moment, Cos invited Rose and his date to join the Poitier party, which included Harry Belafonte.

"Are you sure you're just a schoolteacher?" his date asked Rose, impressed as could be.

The two Bills had been friendly at Temple, but, Rose said, not "buddy-buddy" because of a "generation gap" — he was then 18 while Bill was in his 20's, "a

"I just can't see praying for someone who's kicking you, and I don't want to go where there's tear gas unless I have some tear gas to throw back at them."

man." Had Cosby just said hello at Small's, it would have been enough.

But it's characteristic of Cosby to extend himself for people he likes, people he knew "when," sometimes to the exclusion of others.

"Bill has a funny feeling for the people he knew before he was famous," said Al Carlisle, the public information director at Temple. "He doesn't communicate especially with them, like writing them or picking up the phone, but when he does happen to see them, he just seems to drop everything."

In 1966, for instance, Cosby was the grand marshal of Philadelphia's Thanksgiving Day Parade. The mayor was waiting to see him, and Bill also wanted to meet Santa Claus, "the guy who used to put coal in my stocking."

Ron Miller, the newsman, wanted to do a short feature interview for TV, as a "sidebar" to the story of the parade. He hadn't arranged ahead of time for the interview with Cosby, who was by then an established celebrity, but Cos waved him over and Miller did a lengthy film interview.

An aide reminded Cosby about the VIP's who were waiting elsewhere, but Cos didn't want to cut his old friend short, and indicated the mayor would have to wait and Santa Claus could come to see him.

When Don Council was in his second year of teaching, Cosby was appearing at the Latin Casino in Camden, and came down to Don's school to give a concert.

Cos has invited long-time friends who are not in show business to come visit him in Beverly Hills, and recently a friend from Philadelphia, on vacation with his family, spent 10 days at Cosby's house.

His old schools, like old friends, seem to occupy a very special place in Cosby's affections.

Sometimes by invitation, and sometimes by surprise, he's dropped in on Germantown High to entertain the students and advise: "Stay in school; all the dropouts have the jobs already," emphasizing that he had "made it" despite being a dropout, only because of a special talent. Charles A. Highsmith, auxiliary district superintendent, who was principal of Germantown High when Cosby came back to surprise an assembly, said Cos was able to make points that teachers and parents had long been trying unsuccessfully to make.

"If one kid stays in school because of me," Cosby commented, "it will be worth the trouble."

Bill's brother, Bob, who followed him at Germantown High and starred in football there, was always being referred to by sports writers as "the brother of Bill Cosby." This happened when Bill was playing for Temple, and even more frequently when he became a successful entertainer.

Sensitive to any possible unpleasant feeling Bob might have felt (Bob denies any resentment), Bill convinced a writer to refer to him as "the brother of Bob Cosby" in a story about two performances the comedian was giving at Germantown High for a benefit. To everyone's amusement, the headline read: "Bob Cosby's Brother Bill Is Big Hit at Germantown."

Temple has never been far from Cos' heart — or, for that matter, his chest.

On *I Spy* he once sported a short sleeved white sweatshirt with the words "Temple University" in red letters across the front, and he wore one for a picture on the jacket of his record album, *Why Is There Air?*

Demand for the shirts mushroomed, and the Temple name became better known than ever.

But his promotion of his alma mater wasn't limited to sweatshirts. For example, when Temple opened its Tyler School of Art in Rome, Cos, who was shooting an *I Spy* episode in Italy, dropped by as a surprise guest. He mentioned the university's name in his act and, later, on *I Spy*. He came back for various Temple functions; helped contact athletes Temple was interested in attracting, and pledged the proceeds of the program book sold at his concerts to the Temple scholarship fund.

During the football season after he'd left, he wired George Makris:

"This is the greatest Temple U. team in many, many years. With pride and determination we can bounce back. I'd love to see us do it.

P.S. Mostly pride.

Bill Cosby, Seattle, Wash."

Cosby has a reputation for going out of his way to be nice to children and teenagers.

He's conducted special interview sessions for school editors and others, lingered to give autographs, given benefits for scholarships.

When Cosby heard that a Texas teenager, Buddy Calk, had offered Carlisle a souvenir toad or rattlesnake, he asked, "How come, if he's my fan, you're getting all the horned toads and rattlesnakes? Tell him to send me a horned toad." Buddy did, and Cos sent him a nice thank-you. Then late in 1967 the Eldorado High student called Temple to say his father had offered to treat him to a Christmas present of a three-way phone call with Carlisle in Pennsylvania and

Cosby on the West Coast. Cos agreed to the idea, talked to Buddy for half an hour and helped to give him a most memorable Christmas.

As patient as he may be with young fans, Cosby has his moods and occasional lapses into peevishness. He's sometimes scolded late comers to his concerts publicly, and shown displeasure on other occasions, as when he made his first appearance in Philadelphia in 1964, and the audience he attracted filled only half the Academy of Music.

"I guess like all performers, he's pretty temperamental," his wife has said. "When he gets moody, he goes off by himself and works it out on the basketball courts or goes for a ride in the car."

Cosby, an impulsive, determined man with a will of iron, rarely loses his temper, but when he does he's explosive, as someone who once made an insulting remark about his wife found out.

Other, less abusive, things make him burn.

"I used to be quite gregarious," he said. "I used to say hello to quite a few people if I knew the surroundings, but now I kind of detest doing that sort of thing because if I stop to say hello to one, then it means five and they want something from me." That something is an autograph.

Yet Cosby, who was always "shy about the whole adoration bit," according to a friend, will sometimes go out of his way to sign autographs and talk — as he did for 45 minutes when he saw a group of returned Viet Nam war veterans at one of his concerts.

What he objects to, he explained, is that the request for an autograph often isn't a way of saying, "How you doin'?" but rather "Do something for me."

Cosby said, "You can make people laugh and forget their troubles, but if you don't sign a piece of paper for them, they dislike you; they won't watch you anymore, they won't buy your records."

Bill gets tired listening to people who say, they need, they need, they need, and is disturbed by people lying or people who don't accept him as a human being, which may be one reason he likes to go off and play ball where he's not likely to be recognized.

Cosby isn't "hung up on his success," according to Miller. It has "absolutely not" spoiled him, says Council. To Sheldon Leonard, Cosby is "the warmest, sweetest, most ingratiating human being you can ever meet," while jazz musician Carl Craig compares him to Charlie Brown — "so groovy, he don't have to hit a home run . . . He's so beautiful."

"He's sensitive and personable," says Weintraub. "Bill today is still Bill Cosby."

"I don't think that drugs are necessary, and I don't think drugs will help anybody to find themselves, unless they're definitely sick and then they should do it under a doctor's care. You're looking for something that's going to take you so close to death, it's going to frighten you so you can straighten up? That's sickness."

16

COS' COZY OFFICE

COS AT HOME

One who shares the view that Bill is basically un-
changed by success is his secretary, Mariette Burr,
who's known him four years, from the beginnings of
his stardom on. Her desk is in the anteroom to Bill's
office in the modern two-story Campbell-Silver-Cosby
Corp. building in Beverly Hills, in walking distance of
Bill's home.

On the assumption that you can tell a man by what
he hangs on his wall, a visit is revealing. Mariette has
selected the items that decorate the walls of the anteroom: photos of Bill and such favorites of his as Sheldon Leonard, Muhammed Ali, the Harlem Globetrot-
ters; a certificate of recognition from a high school; a
framed check; a comic book cover, and a letter to
Cosby from Sen. Robert F. Kennedy (who was Cos'
favorite for the presidency), in which the late Senator
referred to the death of Dr. Martin Luther King and his
funeral, which they attended together.

The inner office, where Bill has his desk, is set off by a thick green rug. The memorabilia Bill has selected for the walls there include photos of his wife and children, his mother, Sidney Poitier, and Miles Davis, 12 Negro faces in one frame done by Charles White, and a framed copy of the Emancipation Proclamation. A bronze head of Dr. King rests behind Bill's desk. Giant chess pieces spill over, near a bottle of wine (a gift from his secretary) that he keeps for his friends. Elsewhere, there are sports trophies he's won, narrow shelves of books including *Catch-22*, *How to Play Winning Chess*, and works on Negro history.

Here is where, his secretary said, the quiet comedian likes to have his friends in for lunch, "people who just want you to rap with them."

Spend a few hours with Bill Cosby at home, and all the things that matter to him, that describe him — cars and kids, family and friends, work and recreation — seem to come to the fore.

On an afternoon in August 1968, for example, when a writer came to interview Cos at his home in Beverly Hills, Cosby was seated at the wheel of his Ferrari sports car, which was parked in the circular driveway. Next to him was Erika. He was wearing a green and black Afro shirt, chino pants and boots, and smoking a long cigar. He waved and called a greeting to his interviewer, shook his hand, and then put a comforting arm around his daughter, who was teary-eyed, and kissed her. Talking as if Erika were speaking, Cosby said, "I am crying because there is too much chlorine in the pool."

He mentioned the chlorine to an employee who came to the door, then led his visitor past a bar he keeps stocked for his friends, a pool table, and a fish tank, and into a quiet den that abounds with microphones. He offered soda or coffee. (Bill's a longtime "chain" coffee drinker, avoids drinking anything alcoholic. For one thing, he's seen what drinking has done to the life of someone close to him; for another, as one of his friends explained, "He doesn't have to drink to be in the groove.")

Outside, children laughed and splashed in the pool behind the house, and dogs barked. (Bill has three dogs: a German shepherd named Sab [after a cry in karate] and another dog, and another dog. "I don't know what they are." The second pet is named Boogie and the third, Fat Albert.)

Cosby was back from a grueling series of one-night stands (he'd once done 25 in a row) that had taken him to Portland, Oregon, and Vancouver, Canada, and to Chicago for Operation Breadbasket. That morning, he'd gone to bed at two, awakened at six for a plane ride to Los Angeles, and then to the office, before coming home to a houseful of guests, including his mother, his young brother-in-law, and one of the fellows he grew up with, who was spending his vacation at the Cosbys', with his son.

He had taken his friend to Vegas, Bill said, "and I used myself — Bill Cosby the entertainer — to go and see Andy Griffith, and go backstage and let him say hello to Andy Griffith, and go over and let him meet James Brown, and go on a plane, and I showed him what a hectic schedule I work under. . . ."

That night, other friends would join them and Bill would show a samauri movie. "We'll just enjoy ourselves, man."

Cosby's own pleasures are tremendously varied. He plays pool (has his own table); plays chess, a game he's just picking up again after he learned how in the service (has sets all over); plays basketball whenever and wherever he can. He plays the drums "every once in a while, but not that much. I use it as a surprise for my neighbors." Poker was a passion, but he said he cut that out, and he added, "I don't like pinnochle anymore — until I go back to Philadelphia."

He uses his Sauna bath "whenever I feel fat" (he's 183 pounds now), and swims in his pool, whose dimensions he doesn't know ("I dive across and can just get to the other side").

He's a big movie buff, and he'll often show films at home — football games, basketball games, (some of which he gets from Shrier at Temple), Gary Cooper in *The Westerner*, and Buster Keaton movies. (He tried unsuccessfully to con a relative out of one of the hats worn by the late comedian.)

As might be expected, many of his friends are from comedy or the other worlds he loves . . . Miles Davis, Sidney Poitier (who calls Cos "Sah"), Harry Belafonte, Henry Silver, Cannonball Adderly, a whole host of jazz musicians, Sammy Davis, Wilt Chamberlain, Lou Alcindor, Walter Hazard. Actor Henry Fonda, he said, "is my father. I adopted him and he adopted me."

To Bill, his friend Muhammed Ali is "a fun guy." They forget business when they're together — "you know, we just kinda sit around and blow air . . . that's what friends are for. He brings his wife and child by, and we just sit around and see who can top the other with stories and what not." They do not, he emphasized, meet in the ring.

Since Bill is happiest when he has people around, the Cosbys will often have friends over. When they go out, they may hit four or five places in one evening, which is not surprising for a "night person" like Bill.

What do Cos and his friends do?

"Oh, we take in the things we like — jazz, rhythm and blues, a good football game, a good basketball game, sometimes going to one after another. He religiously goes to Los Angeles Lakers and Rams games, and watches the Philadelphia pro teams whenever he can. Shrier once got a letter from Cosby before a trip to his old hometown, saying he'd like to see the Philadelphia 76'ers Friday, Temple Saturday, and the Eagles Sunday. "That's an idea of his interest in sports," Shrier observed.

Other evidences of his keen interest in sports are the souvenirs, including football shoes, and the way he works out whenever he can. Then there's the answer he gives to the question of who would he be if he could be anyone in the world. His answer: "Gale Sayers because I love football and that's what I really . . . " His voice trailed off.

But he's enjoying his career. "I treat myself pretty good," he said. "I don't punish myself. When I get tired, I go to sleep. When I feel good, I get in there. When I get tired, I take myself away from it."

It was almost time for him to get away from it — to nap until 7:45 when he'd dress for dinner with his friends.

But first, his leg jiggling nervously, a game of chess with his brother-in-law near the pool, and the answer to a basic question. . . .

Since he started making it in the entertainment

world, Cosby has been talking about making a million, going back to college, getting his degree, and then going to teach in one of the poor, tough school districts. ("If I can keep even one confused, unhappy kid from going down the drain, from dropping out of school, I'll have made a real contribution.")

"There aren't too many people in the slums of the type to take a kid with a bright mind and get him to asking questions. I want to be that type."

Will he do it?

Some say a man as successful and earning as much money as Cosby is could never give it up. Others who know him say either that he'll do it, or at least spend a portion of hi᾽ time working with children.

Said Cosby himself. "Looks good, looks very good." Target date: about 1971. (He'll still have to get his degree.) It won't necessarily be Philadelphia (his wife doesn't like the city), but the ideal setup, as far as Bill is concerned, would be:

"Someplace I can teach — I can study, teach, coach. And basically just kind of get up in the morning and look out and see what kind of a day it is and just go."